AF269866

# WNBA *Hot Ticket*

# CONNECTICUT SUN

**To Leo and Dane, the biggest superstars I've ever met.**

The stats and information in this book are accurate through July 2024.




Lerner Publications Company
An imprint of Lerner Publishing Group, Inc.
241 First Avenue North
Minneapolis, MN 55401 USA

For reading levels and more information, look up this title at www.lernerbooks.com.

Main body text set in Aptifer Slab LT Pro / Typeface provided by Linotype AG



**Library of Congress Cataloging-in-Publication Data**

Names: Anderson, Josh, author.
Title: Connecticut Sun / Josh Anderson.
Description: Minneapolis, MN : Lerner Publications, [2025] | Series: WNBA hot ticket (Lerner sports) | Includes bibliographical references and index. | Audience: Ages 7–11 | Audience: Grades 2–3 | Summary: "The Connecticut Sun have reached the WNBA Finals four times, but they have never won the league championship. Meet the players and coaches who fans hope will change the team's fortunes for the better"—Provided by publisher.
Identifiers: LCCN 2024030319 (print) | LCCN 2024030320 (ebook) | ISBN 9798765669723 (library binding) | ISBN 9798765669815 (paperback) | ISBN 9798765669839 (epub)
Subjects: LCSH: Connecticut Sun (Basketball team)—Juvenile literature. | Women's National Basketball Association—Juvenile literature. | Women basketball players—United States—Juvenile literature.
Classification: LCC GV885.52.C66 A53 2025  (print) | LCC GV885.52.C66  (ebook) | DDC 796.323/6409746—dc23/eng/20240702

LC record available at https://lccn.loc.gov/2024030319
LC ebook record available at https://lccn.loc.gov/2024030320

Manufactured in the United States of America
1 – CG – 12/15/24

# TABLE OF CONTENTS

# SUN COMING UP

The third quarter of Game 5 of the 2022 WNBA semifinals had been a complete disaster for the Connecticut Sun. They scored only eight points and allowed the Chicago Sky to score 18. The opening moments of the fourth quarter had barely helped to cut Chicago's lead.

With just under four minutes left in the game, the Sky led by nine points, 63–54. Then the Sun caught fire. Forward DeWanna Bonner made a layup and a free throw to cut the lead to six. Connecticut's 5-foot-8 (1.7 m) guard, Courtney Williams, blocked a three-point attempt and scored a basket. Then the Sun's biggest star, Alyssa Thomas, made two free throws and assisted on a basket to tie the game 63–63. The Sun were rolling.

With exactly two minutes left, Sun center Jonquel Jones was fouled as she hit a layup. Her free throw put Connecticut up 66–63. The Sun's run continued until the game ended. Connecticut won 72–63. They'd held the Sky scoreless for nearly five minutes, ending the game and the series on an 18–0 run.

The Sun lost to the Las Vegas Aces in the WNBA Finals. But Sun fans cheer for one of the most successful teams in the WNBA. The team has a superstar in 2023 WNBA Most Valuable Player (MVP) runner-up Alyssa Thomas. And Connecticut hasn't missed the playoffs since 2016. They made it to at least the league semifinals each season from 2019 to 2023 and played in the Finals twice. Fans hope the team's first championship is right around the corner.

Jonquel Jones played for the Sun from 2016 until 2022.

Courtney Williams (*left*) shakes hands with teammate Alyssa Thomas after Thomas scored a basket against the Sky.

Taj McWilliams-Franklin (*right*) shoots over a Detroit Shock defender during a 1999 game.

The Connecticut Sun began play in 1999 as the Orlando Miracle. In 2003, the Mohegan Tribe bought the team and moved them to Uncasville, Connecticut. The Mohegan Tribe became the first Native American group to own a pro sports team.

The Sun play at Mohegan Sun Arena, located at the Mohegan Sun Casino & Resort. The team's name comes from the name of the resort. Their logo is a modern take on an ancient Mohegan symbol.

Mohegan Sun Arena seats 10,000 fans for Connecticut Sun games.

The Sun were the first WNBA team to play in a state that didn't also have a National Basketball Association team. But fans in Connecticut were used to watching successful women's basketball. In 2003, the University of Connecticut (UConn) Huskies were in the middle of the greatest run in women's college basketball history. They won 11 national championships between 1995 and 2016. The Sun's owners knew Connecticut was full of women's basketball fans.

The Sun became an instant success after their move. They made the playoffs every season from 2003 to 2008. In 2004, they made it all the way to the WNBA Finals for the first time. They lost to the Seattle Storm two games to one in a close series. Connecticut made it back to the Finals in 2005 but lost again, this time to the Sacramento Monarchs.

Nykesha Sales dribbles past a defender during Game 2 of the 2004 WNBA Finals.

Point guard Lindsay Whalen (*left*) played for the Sun from 2004 until 2009.

In the team's early years in Connecticut, coach Mike Thibault relied on several top stars. One was Nykesha Sales, a seven-time All-Star player. She ranks seventh all-time with 1.8 steals per game in her career. Another was Taj McWilliams-Franklin, whose 3,013 rebounds rank ninth in league history. Future Basketball Hall of Famer Lindsay Whalen joined the team in 2004. She played for the Sun for six seasons.

Alyssa Thomas averaged 11.4 points and 1.4 steals per game in her first 10 seasons with the Sun.

The Sun's current period of success started in 2017 under coach Curt Miller. Center Jonquel Jones played for the Sun from 2016 to 2022. She earned five All-Star selections and the league's MVP award in 2021. Alyssa Thomas joined the team in 2014 and became their best player. Thomas is the WNBA's all-time leader in triple-doubles. In 2023, Thomas finished second in MVP voting.

Thomas and her teammates helped the Sun reach the Finals in 2019 and 2022. But the Sun have never won the WNBA championship. After a string of successful seasons, Sun fans hope the team will soon hold the championship trophy.

# WORKING FOR CHANGE

The Sun work hard on the court, but they also work to make a difference in their community. In 2019, the team started a program called Change Can't Wait. The program focuses on wiping out racism in the United States. The Sun partner with local schools, businesses, and community groups. They work with local leaders to help people register to vote and pick candidates who will have a positive impact. The team also hosts events at games to promote Black-owned businesses and raise awareness about racism.

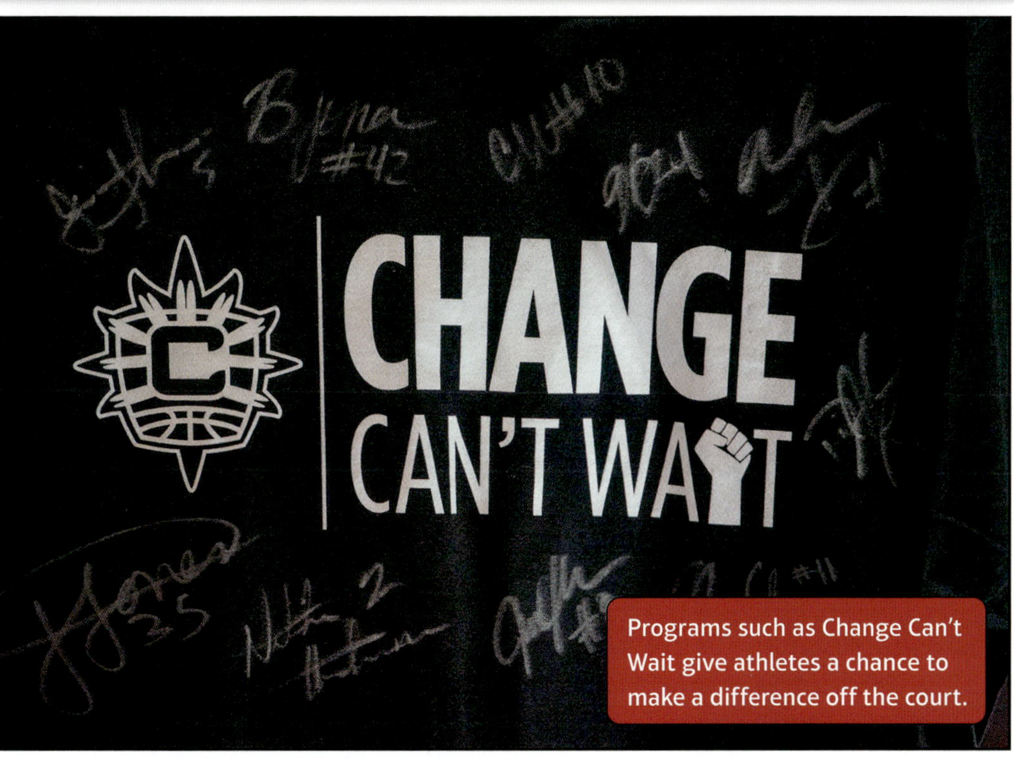


Programs such as Change Can't Wait give athletes a chance to make a difference off the court.

Nykesha Sales (*center*) played 278 games for the Sun. She was one of the WNBA's top-ten scorers during three of her seasons with the team.

# CHAPTER 2

# BRIGHT STARS

Coach Mike Thibault led the Sun teams that were among the best in the WNBA in the early 2000s. Thibault is the team's all-time leader in coaching victories. He led the Sun to the playoffs in eight of his 10 seasons with the team, and to the WNBA Finals twice. His teams were led by a trio of superstars.

Nykesha Sales was a member of the Orlando Miracle and moved with the team to Connecticut. Sales starred at UConn during her college career, so she was a popular player in Connecticut. She played a total of nine seasons with the Sun. A seven-time All-Star, Sales is the Sun's all-time leader in scoring and steals.

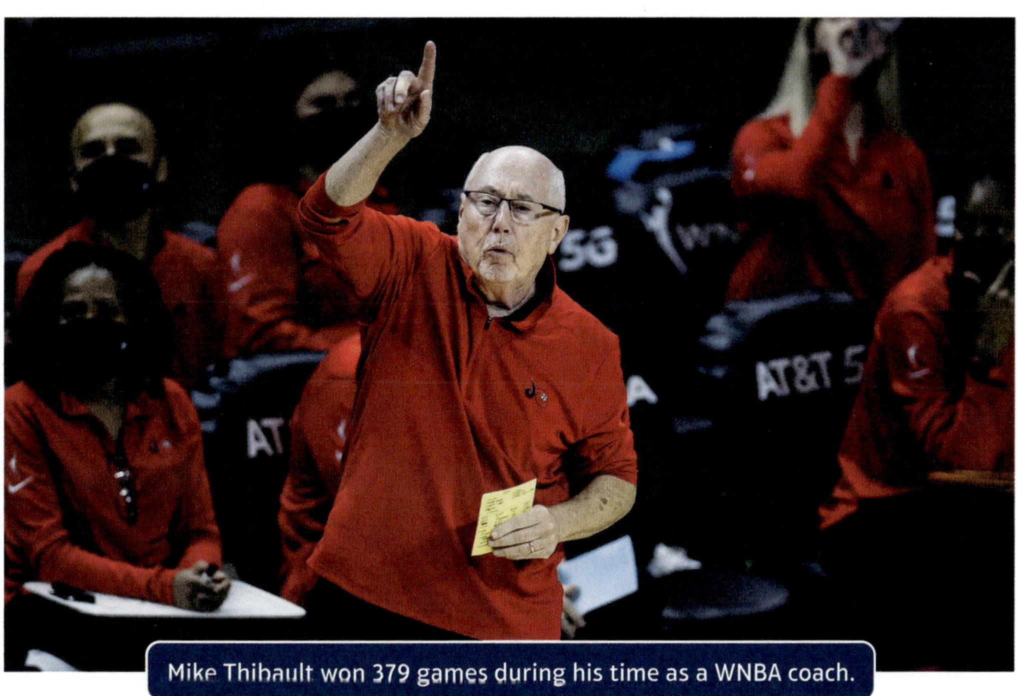

Mike Thibault won 379 games during his time as a WNBA coach.

Sales's top teammates during her time with the Sun were Taj McWilliams-Franklin and Katie Douglas. McWilliams-Franklin played for the team from 1999 to 2006, earning All-Star honors in five of those seasons. She is the team's all-time leader in offensive rebounds and ranks second in total rebounds and blocked shots.

Douglas's 382 three-point baskets are more than any other player in team history. Only five players in league history have hit more three-pointers than Douglas. Douglas also ranks ninth in the league for career steals with 623.

Katie Douglas averaged 1.1 offensive rebounds, 2.7 defensive rebounds, and 1.6 three-pointers per game during her eight seasons with the team.

Lindsay Whalen played the first six seasons of her Hall of Fame career with the Sun. The point guard finished in the top six in assists each season, leading the league in 2007. Whalen went on to be a key part of four title-winning teams with the Minnesota Lynx. She finished her career with 2,345 assists, fourth most in WNBA history.

Before a 2023 trade sent her to the New York Liberty, Jonquel Jones played the first six seasons of her career in Connecticut. She won the Sixth Player of the Year award in 2018 and then earned the league's MVP award in 2021. Jones's 270 blocked shots are the most in team history.

Jonquel Jones dribbles down the court during a 2022 game against the Chicago Sky.

One of the team's best players is DeWanna Bonner. After she spent her first 10 seasons with the Phoenix Mercury, Bonner came to the Sun in a 2020 trade. Bonner improved her scoring average by two points when she joined the Sun. She averaged more than 16 points per game during her time in Connecticut. For her career, the six-time WNBA All-Star ranks fifth in points in league history.

The top star on the roster is Alyssa Thomas. She is a big force on defense and offense. Thomas has ranked in the top 10 in rebounds and steals six times, and in assists five times. She finished as the runner-up in MVP voting in 2023 when she averaged 15.5 points, 9.9 rebounds, and 7.9 assists per game.

Alyssa Thomas shoots a layup over a Minnesota Lynx defender during the 2023 WNBA playoffs.

HOOPS SCOOP
DeWanna Bonner had the highest-scoring game in Sun history in 2023. She scored 41 points against the Las Vegas Aces.

Katie Douglas celebrates the Sun's win over the Seattle Storm in Game 1 of the 2004 WNBA Finals.

# CHAPTER 3

# FINALLY THE FINALS

Taj McWilliams-Franklin was with the team since the beginning. She had played through four seasons in Orlando, all of them with losing records. Orlando had only one playoff appearance to show for their efforts. McWilliams-Franklin moved with the team to Connecticut where they lost in the Eastern Conference Finals in 2003.

Nykesha Sales (*right*) averaged 14.8 points per game during the 2004 WNBA playoffs.

The Sun's chance to stamp their ticket to the 2004 WNBA Finals was on the line in Game 2 of the 2004 Eastern Conference Finals. McWilliams-Franklin was ready. The Sun and New York Liberty traded leads throughout the first half before McWilliams-Franklin hit a three-pointer to put the Sun up 26–25 at halftime.

Early in the second half, after the Sun had fallen behind, McWilliams-Franklin hit a layup to put them back up 35–34. The Liberty surged again and took their largest lead of the half, 42–37. Then McWilliams-Franklin hit back-to-back layups to bring the Sun within one.

Taj McWilliams-Franklin (*left*) played for five other WNBA teams after her eight seasons with the Sun.

McWilliams-Franklin (*leaping in white*) scored 83 points and grabbed 59 total rebounds for the Sun during the 2004 WNBA playoffs.

With only 48 seconds left, she was on the free throw line with the score tied 54–54. McWilliams-Franklin's free throw put the Sun up for good. The 60–57 victory sent Connecticut to its first WNBA Finals. McWilliams-Franklin's 18 points and nine rebounds led the team.

Jasmine Thomas (*right*) celebrates her three-pointer during Game 1 of the 2019 WNBA semifinals.

The next season, the Sun faced the Indiana Fever in Game 2 of the Eastern Conference Finals. After the Sun took a 37–29 lead into halftime, they looked to be on their way to a victory. But the Fever stormed back. WNBA legend Tamika Catchings hit a three-pointer for Indiana to tie the game in the final seconds, sending the contest to overtime. In overtime, the Sun outscored the Fever 17–8 to earn their second straight trip to the Finals.

Fourteen years later, the Sun were one game away from the Finals again. This time, their opponent was the Los Angeles Sparks. Game 3 of that series wouldn't need overtime, though. Led by Jasmine Thomas's 29 points and Courtney Williams's 17, the game was an easy 78–56 Sun victory.

Courtney Williams dribbles past Los Angeles Sparks defender Marina Mabrey during the 2019 season.

Alyssa Thomas led the WNBA in assists during the 2023 WNBA season.

# CHAPTER 4

# A BRIGHT FUTURE

The Sun have been knocking on the door of a WNBA title for almost 10 years. After taking the Sun to their second Finals appearance in four seasons, coach Curt Miller left to take the same position for the Los Angeles Sparks. The Sun hired Stephanie White before the 2023 season, and she led them to a 27–13 finish in her first year in Connecticut. That's the most wins in a season in team history. The Sun lost in the WNBA semifinal playoff round. But White still won the league's Coach of the Year award.

Before becoming a coach, Stephanie White (*left*) played five seasons in the WNBA. She joined the Sun in 2023.

Only the New York Liberty have appeared in the playoffs and WNBA Finals more often without a championship than the Sun. No team has won more regular-season games without winning a title than Connecticut. With stars such as Brionna Jones and DeWanna Bonner on the roster, and a yearly MVP candidate in Alyssa Thomas, the Sun have the players to compete for a title. Sun fans have seen the team achieve winning seasons and reach the Finals, and now they want more. Whether Coach White can get them there will determine if this era of Sun basketball can be truly historic.

DeWanna Bonner (*left*) ranks in the WNBA's top 10 in multiple stats, including free throws made, total rebounds, and steals.

Brionna Jones won the WNBA's Most Improved Player award in 2021 and the Sixth Player of the Year award in 2022.

# GLOSSARY

**assist:** a pass that leads directly to a basket

**free throw:** an open shot taken from behind a set line after a foul by an opponent

**layup:** a shot in basketball made from near the basket, usually by playing the ball off the backboard

**overtime:** an extra period played at the end of a game that is tied

**playoffs:** games held after the season to determine each year's champion

**rebound:** grabbing and controlling the ball after a missed shot

**roster:** a list of players on a team

**semifinal:** a game or a series of games coming before the final round in a tournament

**sixth player:** a team's top player who is not on the floor at the start of the game

**steal:** when a basketball player takes the ball from an opposing player

**triple-double:** when a player reaches at least 10 in three different stats categories in a game

# LEARN MORE

Connecticut Sun
https://sun.wnba.com/

Doeden, Matt. *G.O.A.T. Women's Basketball Teams*. Minneapolis: Lerner Publications, 2021.

Leed, Percy. *Pro Basketball by the Numbers*. Minneapolis: Lerner Publications, 2025.

Whiting, Jim. *The Story of the Connecticut Sun*. Mankato, MN: Creative Education and Creative Paperbacks, 2024.

WNBA
https://www.wnba.com/

Women's National Basketball Association Facts for Kids
https://kids.kiddle.co/Women%27s_National_Basketball
_Association

# INDEX



# PHOTO ACKNOWLEDGMENTS


Image credits: Image credits: Michael Reaves/Getty Images Sport/Getty Images, p.4; Michael Reaves/Getty Images Sport/Getty Images, p.6; Michael Reaves/Getty Images Sport/Getty Images, p.7; Eliot J. Schechter/Allsport/Getty Images, p.8; Maddie Meyer/Getty Images Sport/Getty Images, p.9; Jeff Vinnick/Getty Images Sport/Getty Images, p.10; Jeff Vinnick/Getty Images Sport/Getty Images, p.11; Alex Slitz/Getty Images Sport/Getty Images, p.12; Erica Denhoff/Icon Sportswire/Getty Images, p.13; Jed Jacobsohn/Getty Images Sport/Getty Images, p.14; Scott Taetsch/Getty Images Sport/Getty Images, p.15; Christian Petersen/Getty Images Sport/Getty Images, p.16; Michael Reaves/Getty Images Sport/Getty Images, p.17; David Berding/Getty Images Sport/Getty Images, p.18; Elsa/Getty Images Sport/Getty Images, p.19; Chris Trotman/Getty Images Sport/Getty Images, p.20; Jed Jacobsohn/Getty Images Sport/Getty Images, p.21; Chris Trotman/Getty Images Sport/Getty Images, p.22; Chris Trotman/Getty Images Sport/Getty Images, p.23; M. Anthony Nesmith/Icon Sportswire/Getty Images, p.24; M. Anthony Nesmith/Icon Sportswire/Getty Images, p.25; Ethan Miller/Getty Images Sport/Getty Images, p.26; Elsa/Getty Images Sport/Getty Images, p.27; Alex Slitz/Getty Images Sport/Getty Images, p.28; Alex Slitz/Getty Images Sport/Getty Images, p.29

Cover image: M. Anthony Nesmith/Icon Sportswire/Getty Images